Cross Stitch
FLOWERS

Cross Stitch
FLOWERS

Over 200 flower-inspired charts for cross stitch

Kandour Ltd

Published by
Kandour Ltd
1-3 Colebrooke Place
London N1 8HZ
UNITED KINGDOM

This edition printed in 2006
for Bookmart Ltd
Registered Number 2372865
Trading as Bookmart Ltd
Blaby Road
Wigston
Leicester LE18 4SE

First published 2006

10 9 8 7 6 5 4 3 2 1

Author: Sue Whiting
Design and art direction: Cutting Edge Media
Production: Karen Lomax

Printed and bound in China
ISBN 1-904756-56-5

Contents

Romantic Roses

*Create pretty pictures of classic full-blown roses to adorn your home.
Make all four and hang them all together, or embroider just one to remind
you of your favourite flowers*

Worked on a 14 count fabric, each rose will be just under 10 cm (4 ins) in diameter.

Choose a simple circular mount card and classic wooden frame as shown here - the roses are so beautiful you won't need anything more!

Our roses are worked on a classic white fabric, with a matching colour mount. But you could choose a mount colour to tone in with your decor. Or you could even work them on a coloured fabric - but make sure you choose a colour that will allow the embroidery to show up clearly.

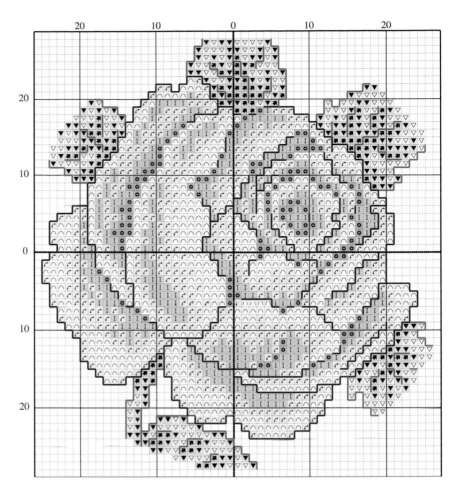

PINKY RED ROSE KEY

	Anchor	DMC	Madeira	
★ Cross stitch in two strands				
↱	24	761	0404	dusky pink
+	26	957	0408	pink
◩	41	602	0702	dark pink
✸	217	367	1312	dark green
▼	242	702	1306	green
▽	259	772	1604	light green
⌒	271	818	0502	baby pink
✛	275	746	2511	cream
C	293	727	0110	light yellow
⊙	306	3852	2509	gold
♥	1006	304	0511	red
★ Backstitch in one strand				
——	683	890	1314	bottle green
——	1006	304	0511	red
★ STITCH COUNT - 56 high x 51 wide				

Our rose embroideries have been made up into a pretty set of pictures to hang on the wall, each with its own neat frame and circular mount. Hang them in a row, either vertically or horizontally, or form them into a square.

You don't have to make all four - choose your favourite and make just one for that special corner of a room. Or make a pair to hang on the wall above a vase of roses.

You could use these motifs to decorate a cushion cover, or a tablecloth. Or add a really special touch to your bed linen by working a rose in the corner of your pillowcase. Whatever they are used for, they will bring a touch of romance to your home!

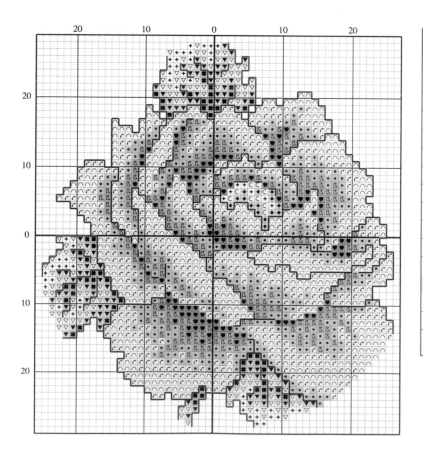

DOG ROSE KEY

★ Cross stitch in two strands

	Anchor	DMC	Madeira	
↶	62	3805	0702	bright pink
+	65	915	0705	dark pink
◩	211	562	1206	dark green
✹	266	470	1503	green
∩	271	818	0502	baby pink
▽	278	3819	2703	lime green
∩	300	745	0111	light yellow
+	305	726	0109	yellow
C	308	782	2211	dark gold
•●•	1094	605	0613	light pink

★ Backstitch in one strand

	65	915	0705	dark pink
——	862	935	1505	bottle green

★ **STITCH COUNT** - 56 high x 51 wide

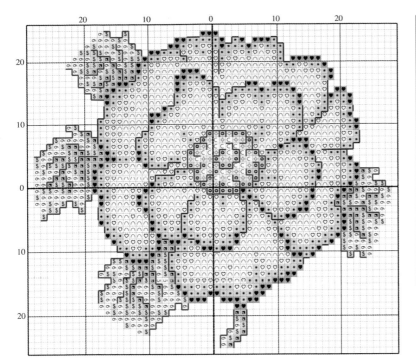

PINK CABBAGE ROSE KEY

★ Cross stitch in two strands

	Anchor	DMC	Madeira	
▽	206	966	1209	light green
▼	242	702	1306	green
∩	271	818	0502	light pink
↗	877	502	1703	dark green
↶	894	152	2310	dusky pink
✪	897	902	0601	very dark pink
I	1024	3328	0401	salmon pink

★ Backstitch in one strand

| —— | 218 | 319 | 1313 | holly green |
| —— | 897 | 902 | 0601 | very dark pink |

★ STITCH COUNT - 56 high x 51 wide

YELLOW ROSE KEY

★ Cross stitch in two strands

	Anchor	DMC	Madeira	
▼	211	562	1206	dark green
$	266	470	1503	green
+	275	746	2511	cream
▽	278	3819	2703	lime green
C	293	727	0110	light yellow
+	298	972	0107	dark yellow
C	304	741	0202	orange
-•-	1004	921	0312	dark copper

★ Backstitch in one strand

| —— | 862 | 935 | 1505 | bottle green |
| —— | 1004 | 921 | 0312 | dark copper ★ |

★ STITCH COUNT - 56 high x 51 wide

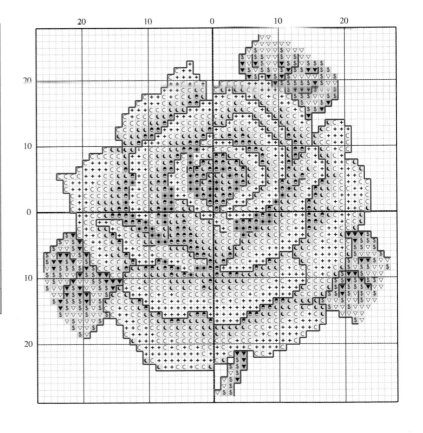

Perfect Poppies

Full blown poppies will bring back happy memories of long hot summer days. Choose from the masterpiece picture, shown above, or one of the quick-makes, shown opposite

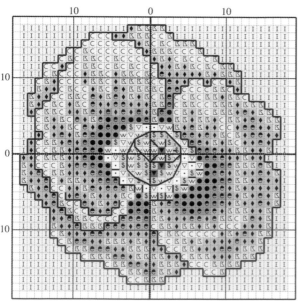

Above: Make this stunning poppy picture to remind you of summer. The chart is on the next page.

Top left: If you want a quick project, why not try this clever little paperweight or the bright greeting card? The paperweight chart is shown left, and the chart for the card is shown on the following page.

Worked on 14 count fabric, the design shown left is about 6 cm (2½ ins) in diameter.

Featuring just one full blown poppy bloom, you could use this design on a greeting card too! Or why not try working it using waste canvas to decorate the pocket of a blouse?

The key for this chart is on the next page.

POPPIES KEY

★ **Cross stitch in two strands**

	DMC	Anchor	Madeira	
∩	blanc	2	2402	white
−	ecru	926	2404	ecru
■	310	403	2400	black
✈	347	1025	0407	dark red
★	350	11	0213	red
☆	351	10	0214	light red
♡	352	9	2605	coral
×	353	6	2605	light coral
Κ	644	830	1814	stone grey
ᔕ	676	891	2208	sand
я	677	886	2207	light sand
▽	704	237	1308	bright green
☾	729	890	2209	dark sand
∨	772	259	1604	lt pine green
-●-	782	308	2212	dark gold
✖	815	44	0513	burgundy
♥	817	13	0210	poppy red
▼	937	268	1504	dark green
◗	3347	266	1408	green
ᔓ	3348	264	1409	light green
◥	3802	1019	0601	dark plum

★ **Backstitch in one strand**

	DMC	Anchor	Madeira	
——	310	403	2400	black
——	782	308	2212	dark gold
——	815	44	0513	burgundy
——	937	268	1504	dark green

★ **French knots in two strands**

●	blanc	2	2402	white

★ **STITCH COUNT** 108 high x 109 wide

The key for the picture chart (right), greeting card chart (below) and paperweight chart (on previous page).

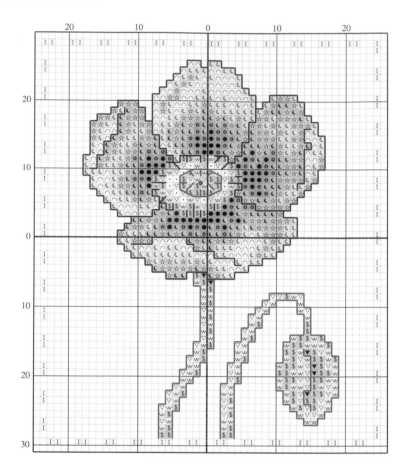

Worked on a 14 count fabric, the design is just over 10 cm (4 ins) tall and about 9 cm (3½ ins) wide.

It's such a pretty bloom it would almost be a shame to give it away! Why not make another one to keep yourself and frame it as a tiny picture?

Above: The chart for the stunning framed picture shown on the previous page.

Worked on a 14 count fabric, the completed design is about 20 cm (8 ins) square.

Our picture was worked on a white fabric but why not try a soft green fabric to create the effect shown on the chart above? But make sure you choose a shade of green that will mean the green of the embroidery will still show up well. Alternatively, if you cannot find the correct shade of soft green, you could always fill in the background by working cross stitch using green thread.

This is such a wonderfully intricate design it is best suited to a simple frame. The clean crisp lines of our white mount board and pale angular frame perfectly compliment the delicate and detailed blooms. To create a far more striking effect, you could try using a brightly coloured frame, picking out one of the colours within the embroidery.

Spring Flowers

Make it spring all year round with these six sumptuous springtime designs. Choose from the aconite or violets shown here, or the crocuses, irises, snowdrops or auricula shown on the following pages

WINTER ACONITE KEY

★ **Cross stitch in two strands**

	Anchor	DMC	Madeira	
✳	218	319	1314	dark green
×	255	907	1310	bright green
▼	258	905	1412	green
▽	278	3819	2703	lime green
⋄	290	444	0106	yellow
C	293	727	0110	light yellow
●	314	741	0202	orange
+	926	ecru	2101	ecru

★ **Backstitch in one strand**

	Anchor	DMC	Madeira	
——	218	319	1314	dark green
——	309	781	2213	tan

★ **STITCH COUNT** - 50 high x 51 wide

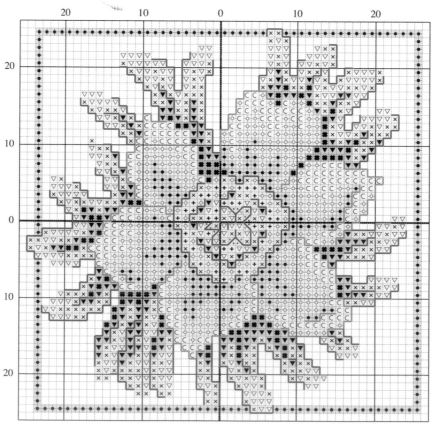

VIOLETS KEY

★ **Cross stitch in two strands**

	Anchor	DMC	Madeira	
♡	96	3608	0709	heather
■	101	550	0714	dark mauve
e	103	3609	0710	light lilac
⌐	110	333	0903	purple
✱	218	319	1314	dark green
▼	245	700	1302	green
▽	254	166	1409	lime green
$	256	906	1411	bright green
-◇-	290	444	0106	yellow
-●-	314	741	0202	orange

★ **Backstitch in one strand**

	Anchor	DMC	Madeira	
——	101	550	0714	dark mauve
——	218	319	1314	dark green

★ **STITCH COUNT** - 51 high x 51 wide

Worked on 14 count fabric, all six designs are just over 9 cm (3½ ins) square, making them perfect to frame as mini pictures. Work all six and hang them in a group, or just make your favourite. You could always make the others at a later date. Perhaps during those long dark winter nights to remind you of the coming spring?

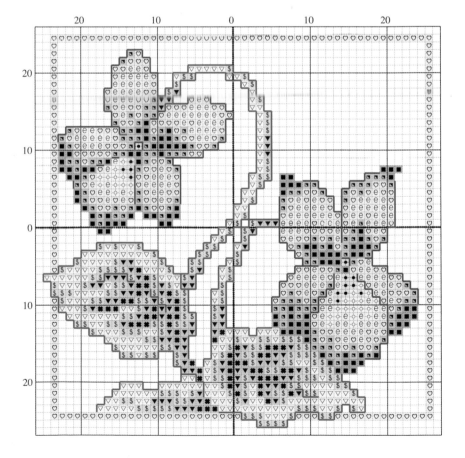

PRIMULA AURICULA KEY

★ **Cross stitch in two strands**

	Anchor	DMC	Madeira	
·	1	B5200	2401	white
♡	25	3716	0606	dark pink
∩	48	963	0503	light pink
♥	57	602	0702	pink
●	65	915	0705	dark fuchsia
�	218	319	1314	dark green
▼	244	987	1206	green
▽	254	166	1409	lime green
$	256	906	1411	bright green
∽	259	772	1604	light green
+	926	ecru	2101	ecru

★ **Backstitch in one strand**

——	65	915	0705	dark fuchsia
——	218	319	1314	dark green

★ **STITCH COUNT** - 51 high x 52 wide

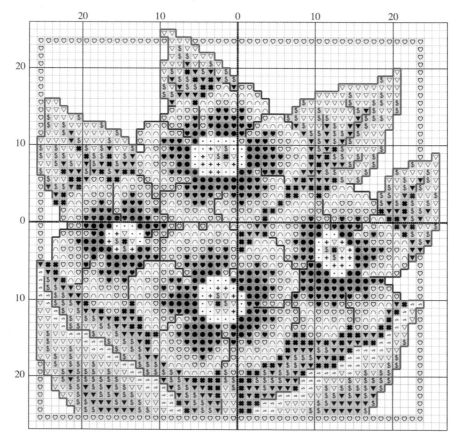

Auriculas can sometimes be difficult to grow - but you're guaranteed success without green fingers for these blooms!

IRIS KEY

★ **Cross stitch in two strands**

	Anchor	DMC	Madeira	
●	65	915	0705	dark fuchsia
♡	96	3608	0709	heather
℮	99	552	0712	mauve
e	103	3609	0710	light lilac
✹	218	319	1314	dark green
▼	244	987	1206	green
▽	254	166	1409	lime green
$	256	906	1411	bright green
∩	271	818	0502	light pink
A	298	972	0107	yellow

★ **Backstitch in one strand**

	Anchor	DMC	Madeira	
——	70	154	2607	dark mauve
——	218	319	1314	dark green

★ **STITCH COUNT** - 52 high x 51 wide

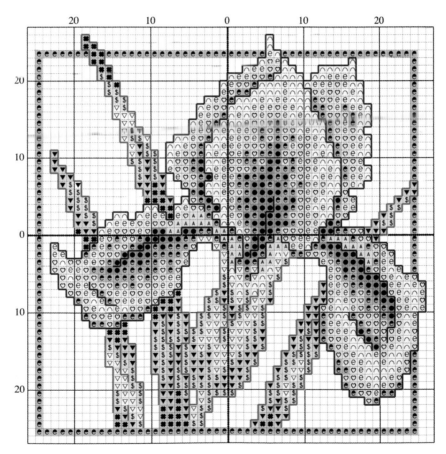

Classic irises are one of our all-time favourite flowers. They're a definite must in every garden - even one that's stitched!

SNOWDROPS KEY

★ Cross stitch in two strands

	Anchor	DMC	Madeira	
·	1	B5200	2401	white
×	225	703	1307	bright green
▼	244	987	1206	green
◊	253	165	1414	lime green
◨	398	415	1802	grey
∽	847	928	1805	light grey
+	926	ecru	2101	ecru

★ Backstitch in one strand

	Anchor	DMC	Madeira	
——	212	561	1205	dark green
——	400	317	1713	dark grey

★ STITCH COUNT - 50 high x 52 wide

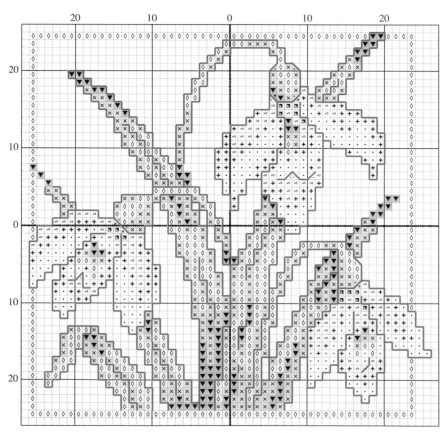

The first herald of spring - the snowdrop! Once these little beauties poke their heads out from the frozen earth we all know spring is not far away.

CROCUSES KEY

★ **Cross stitch in two strands**

	Anchor	DMC	Madeira	
e	8	3824	0304	peach
⊕	42	309	0508	dark pink
●	89	917	0706	dark magenta
▽	203	955	1210	light green
C	275	746	2511	cream
t	292	3078	0102	light yellow
-◇-	297	973	0106	yellow
▼	879	500	1705	dark green
e	895	223	0812	dusky pink
♦	1074	992	1202	turquoise

★ **Backstitch in one strand**

——	879	500	1705	dark green
—	1029	154	2607	cerise

★ **STITCH COUNT** - 51 high x 53 wide

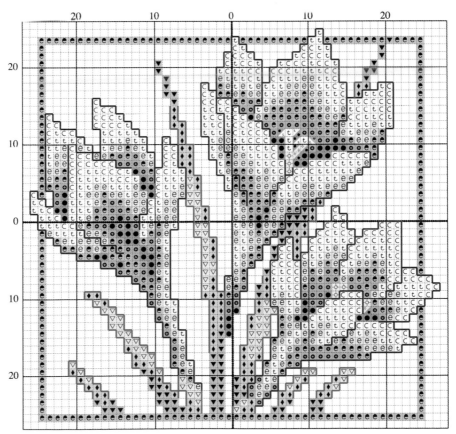

Spring has truly arrived when the crocuses are out. Remember those magnificent carpets of their bright shiny heads waving in the gentle spring breezes?

FLORAL ABC KEY

★ **Cross stitch in two strands**

	DMC	Anchor	Madeira	
I	210	108	0802	lilac
3	340	118	0902	violet blue
◣	550	102	0714	dark mauve
♭	704	237	1308	bright green
⌒	722	323	0307	ginger
☆	725	291	0113	yellow
-◇-	727	293	0110	light yellow
♭	922	1003	2306	copper
♂	959	186	1114	mint green
♀	3608	86	0709	pink
♡	3689	74	0606	light pink
♥	3805	57	0702	dark pink
+	3819	278	2703	moss green
C	3823	386	2511	cream
▼	3837	111	2710	dark lilac

★ **Backstitch in one strand**

——	917	89	0706	magenta
——	3850	189	1203	jade green

★ **STITCH COUNT** 132 high x 104 wide

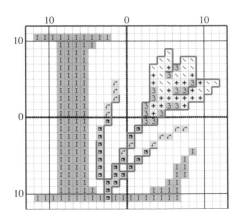

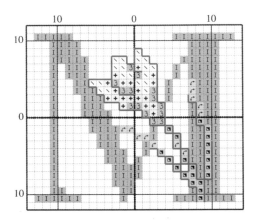

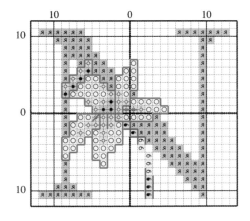

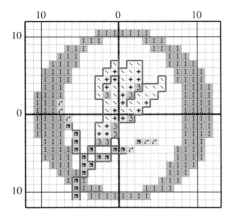

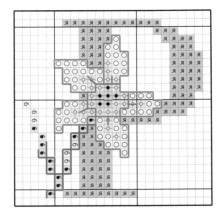

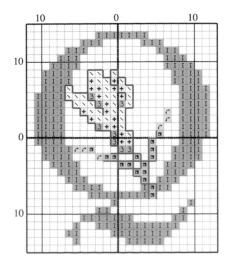

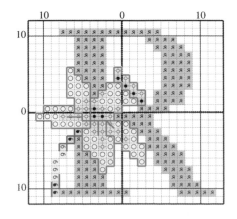

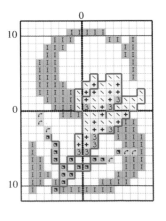

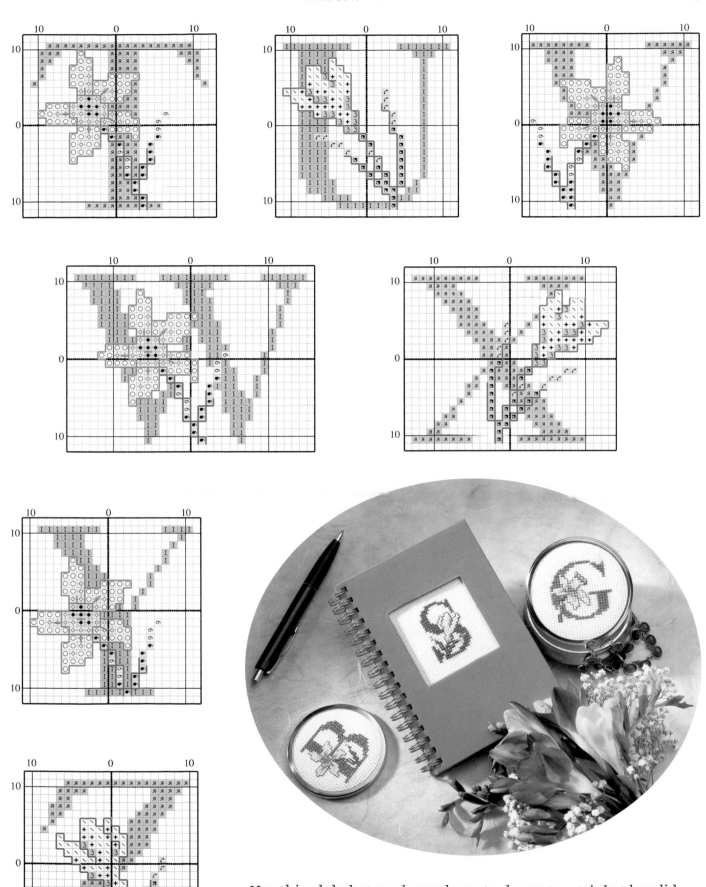

Use this alphabet as shown here, to decorate a trinket box lid, a little coaster or a handy note book. Or work one in the corner of a handkerchief, or on a greeting card. Try personalising a garment by working the letter through waste canvas onto the pocket of a blouse or nightdress, or onto a baby's bib for a special occasion. The possibilities are endless!

Oriental Inspiration

Bring a touch of the orient into your home with these stunning designs, inspired by eastern delights. Choose from peonies in a picture, a delicate butterfly that's settled on a trinket box or cherry blossom on a greeting card

ORIENTAL BLOOMS KEY

★ **Cross stitch in two strands**

	Anchor	DMC	Madeira	
˅	9	352	0303	coral
♥	11	350	0212	dark coral
♡	24	3326	0404	light pink
✳	76	3731	0603	dark pink
▽	203	955	1210	light green
⦿	218	319	1314	dark green
◊	254	166	1409	lime green
↶	259	772	1604	very lt green
✸	263	520	1405	bottle green
▼	267	470	1503	moss green
/\	271	819	0501	very light pink
၅	279	166	1501	lt olive green
C	301	744	0112	yellow
╲	386	3823	2511	cream
✪	844	3012	1606	olive green
×	877	502	1703	pine green
●	1006	304	0511	dark red
⌒	1042	504	1309	lt pine green

★ **Backstitch in one strand**

——	11	350	0212	dark coral
——	218	319	1314	dark green
——	263	520	1405	bottle green
——	846	936	1507	dk olive green
——	972	3803	2609	dark plum
——	1006	304	0511	dark red

★ **STITCH COUNT** - 112 high x 112 wide

Make a butterfly to settle on your trinket box using this little chart - or scatter them over a cushion or pillowcase.

Worked on a 14 count fabric, the butterfly is just under 4 cm (1½ ins) in both directions. You don't have to stick to just the pinks we used for the butterfly's wings - choose any colours you want and make it as bright or subtle as you wish.

Left: This key is for the butterfly and cherry blossom charts shown here, and for the picture chart shown overleaf.

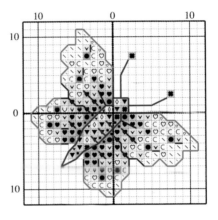

Left: The chart for the cherry blossom design shown on the greeting card - but it's so pretty you could easily frame it and use it as a little picture!

Worked on 14 count fabric, the design is just over 5 cm (2 ins) square.

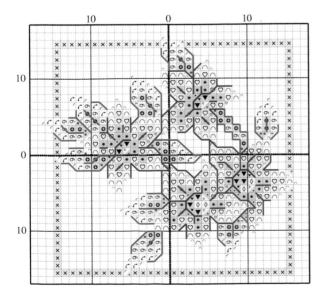

Bright Flowers

Make greeting cards for all and every occasion with these bright floral designs. Each pretty flower sits inside a coloured frame and there are seven to choose from - that's one for every day of the week!

Choose from one of these seven little flower designs - the poppy and daisy shown here, and the pansy, rose, lily, sunflower and clematis designs shown on the following four pages. Each one would make a beautiful greeting card to send to a close friend or family member.

You could make the full set and then applique them onto a cushion cover to create a patchwork effect. Or buy a picture mount board

with several apertures and make a little flower motif to sit behind each opening and create a row of flowers - choose different flowers or repeat the same motif to form a jolly row of blooms.

Worked on 14 count fabric, each motif is about 5 cm (2 ins) square. The key for all the designs is shown on the opposite page.

DAISY KEY

★ **Cross stitch in two strands**

	Anchor	DMC	Madeira	
+	1	B5200	2401	white
v	234	762	1804	light grey
I	254	472	1308	light green
▼	266	470	1502	green
⋄	288	445	0103	light yellow
●	298	972	0107	yellow

★ **Backstitch in one strand**

——	400	317	1713	grey
——	861	935	1508	dark green

★ **STITCH COUNT** 30 high x30 wide

POPPY KEY

★ **Cross stitch in two strands**

	Anchor	DMC	Madeira	
♥	46	666	0210	red
▽	254	472	1308	light green
☆	330	947	0205	orange
■	403	310	2400	black
♡	1019	315	0810	dark plum
N	1090	996	1103	electric blue

★ **Backstitch in one strand**

——	403	310	2400	black
——	1005	816	0513	dark red

★ **STITCH COUNT** 30 high x30 wide

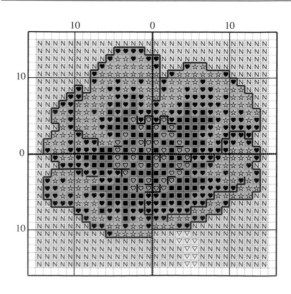

Above: Choose a simple but cheery daisy! Set inside a green card, with a toning green background to the motif, this one would be ideal to send to a teenager.

Set off to perfection by the red greeting card, here's a classic full-blown red poppy sitting against a blue sky to remind you of summer!

ROSE KEY

	Anchor	DMC	Madeira	
★ **Cross stitch in two strands**				
◊	25	3716	0606	pink
♦	38	956	0702	dark pink
∩	48	963	0503	light pink
♥	59	150	0509	cherry red
K	117	157	0907	blue
★ **Backstitch in one strand**				
——	59	150	0509	cherry red
★ **STITCH COUNT** 30 high x30 wide				

Above: One perfect rose set against a blue background inside the prettiest of pink cards - the perfect gift for a loved one!

This rose is so beautiful, why restrict its use to just a greeting card? Using waste canvas, embroider just the rose motif itself, omitting the background area, sprinkled over simple crisp white bedding to create the ultimate bed of roses. Or scatter roses over an evening shawl, or work the design onto the front of a pair of satin slippers and make a matching bag.

Right: The chart for the rose card above. The key is shown on the previous page.

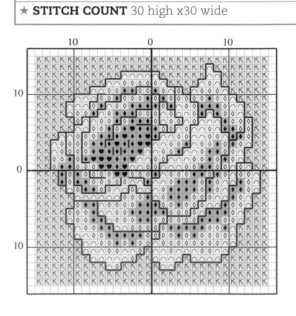

PANSY KEY

★ **Cross stitch in two strands**

	Anchor	DMC	Madeira	
I	36	3326	0504	pink
✪	101	550	00713	dark mauve
e	108	210	2711	light mauve
●	110	208	2711	mauve
●	177	792	0905	blue
○	298	972	0107	yellow

★ **Backstitch in one strand**

	Anchor	DMC	Madeira	
——	101	550	00713	dark mauve

★ **STITCH COUNT** 30 high x30 wide

Below: Pansy: from the french "pense" - to think. Let your friends know you think of them by making this card to send with love.

This card combines pinks and soft purples to create a very pretty, feminine card, but you could make it much brighter by replacing the background shade of soft pink with a much more intense colour. How about a strong yellow to match the pansy's eye?

To make a matching gift, why not embroider the same pansy design onto a little pot pourri sachet? Or inset one inside the top of a trinket box, or a paperweight.

Left: The chart for the pansy card shown below. The key is on the previous page.

A glowing lily to send with warmth and love. Match your greeting card to the golden tones of the flower to make it really stand out! And don't limit this design to just a greeting card - why not use some metallic threads within the embroidery and work this motif onto a glamorous golden evening purse?

LILY KEY

★ **Cross stitch in two strands**

	Anchor	DMC	Madeira	
✪	101	550	00713	dark mauve
◨	176	793	0905	blue
☾	303	742	0101	light orange
☆	311	3855	2014	orange
★	330	947	0205	dark orange
♭	1043	369	2306	green

★ **Backstitch in one strand**

	Anchor	DMC	Madeira	
——	211	562	1206	dark green
——	1025	347	0508	dark red

★ **STITCH COUNT** 30 high x30 wide

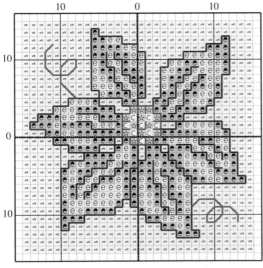

CLEMATIS KEY

★ **Cross stitch in two strands**

	Anchor	DMC	Madeira	
e	90	554	0711	light mauve
●	98	553	0712	mauve
C	301	744	0112	yellow
☆	306	3820	2514	dark yellow
∽	1094	964	1112	green

★ **Backstitch in one strand**

	Anchor	DMC	Madeira	
——	101	550	0713	dark mauve
——	277	830	2114	khaki

★ **STITCH COUNT** 30 high x30 wide

One perect clematis bloom, set against a watery blue background inside a matching greeting card.

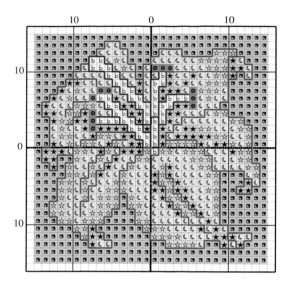

SUNFLOWER KEY

★ Cross stitch in two strands			
	Anchor	DMC	Madeira
▪	109	155	0902	lilac
C	288	445	0103	light yellow
-◇-	298	972	0107	yellow
✪	309	781	2213	old gold
●	359	801	2006	brown
★ Backstitch in one strand			
——	309	781	2213	old gold
——	381	938	2005	dark brown
★ STITCH COUNT 30 high x30 wide			

The brightest of sunflowers, worked against a clear sky blue and set into a jolly matching yellow card. The perfect card to send for a summer birthday! Why not send a big bunch of real sunflowers too? Just think how wonderful this little card will look sitting in front of the vase - and it will become a lasting memory of those summer flowers that fade all too fast.

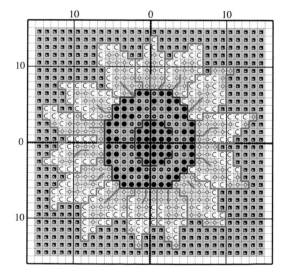

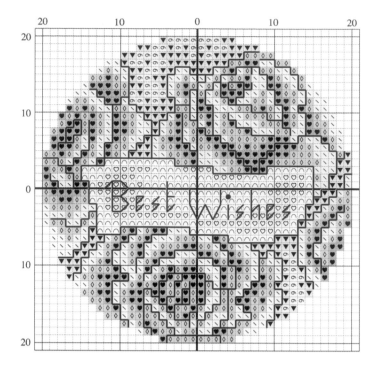

The chart for the red rose design, shown top right in the photograph.

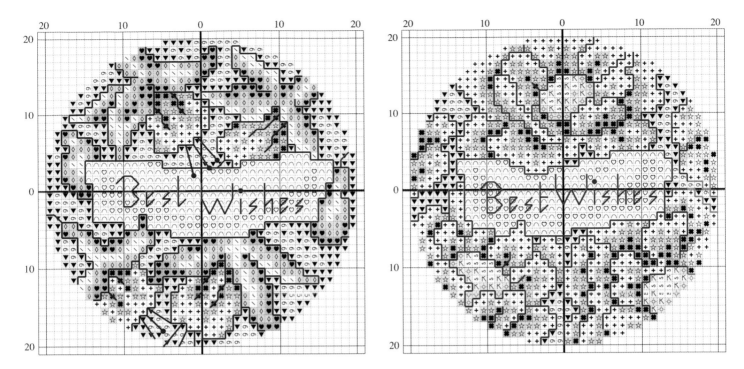

BEST WISHES CARDS KEY

★ **Cross stitch in two strands**

	Anchor	DMC	Madeira	
◊	10	351	0214	light red
\	24	3326	0404	light pink
♥	46	666	0210	red
+	48	963	0503	very lt pink
☆	66	3806	0701	light plum
✖	68	3607	0708	plum
๑	240	3348	1414	light green
▼	242	702	1306	green
K	291	444	0106	yellow
ى	293	727	0110	light yellow
⋄	303	742	0201	tangerine
↗	330	947	0207	dark orange
∩	926	712	2102	cream
♡	933	543	1909	beige

★ **Backstitch in one strand**

	Anchor	DMC	Madeira	
——	43	815	0513	dark red

★ **French knots in one strand**

	Anchor	DMC	Madeira	
●	43	815	0513	dark red

★ **STITCH COUNT** - 40 high x 40 wide

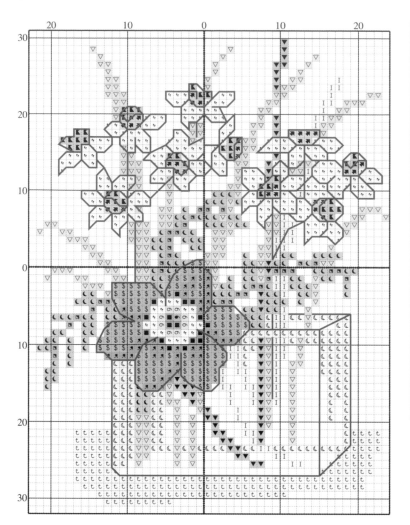

FLOWER ARRANGEMENT KEY

★ **Cross stitch in two strands**

	DMC	Anchor	Madeira	
Ꞩ	165	278	1414	light green
■	310	403	2400	black
⬈	347	13	0407	dark red
$	349	1098	0212	red
◪	562	209	1213	sea green
▽	704	255	1308	green
◤	741	304	0202	dark orange
⬈	742	303	0201	orange
▼	905	257	1412	dark green
◓	924	851	1706	dk petrol blue
◓	926	850	1707	petrol blue
I	966	206	1209	lt sea green
☾	3811	1060	1101	turquoise
ʈ	3823	300	0111	cream
☾	3838	176	2702	blue

★ **Backstitch in one strand**

——	926	850	1707	petrol blue

★ **STITCH COUNT** - 61 high x 47 wide

HYACINTH KEY

★ **Cross stitch in two strands**

	DMC	Anchor	Madeira	
N	155	1030	0803	light purple
Ꞩ	165	278	1414	light green
＼	210	108	0802	lilac
★	333	119	0903	purple
☆	340	118	0902	violet
▽	704	255	1308	green
∽	775	1031	1014	light blue
▼	905	257	1412	dark green
I	966	206	1209	lt sea green
☾	3811	1060	1101	turquoise

★ **Backstitch in one strand**

——	333	119	0903	purple
——	926	850	1707	petrol blue

★ **STITCH COUNT** - 57 high x 40 wide

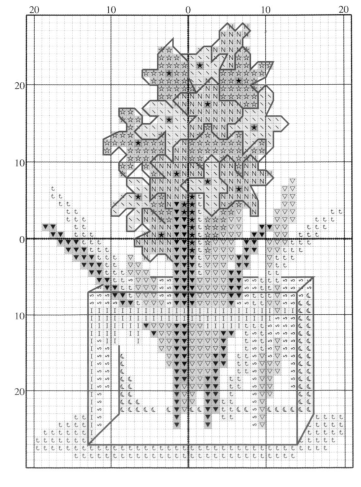

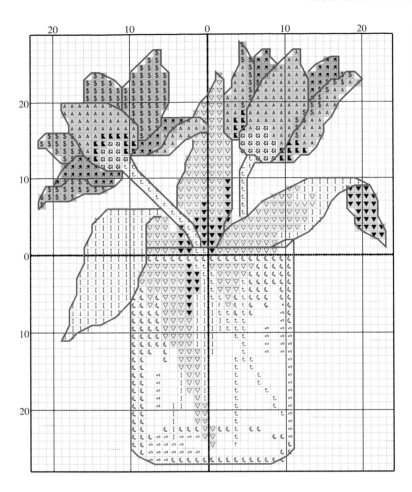

TULIPS KEY

★ **Cross stitch in two strands**

	DMC	Anchor	Madeira	
t	165	278	1414	light green
⊅	347	13	0407	dark red
$	349	1098	0212	red
A	351	10	0214	light red
▽	704	255	1308	green
◤	741	304	0202	dark orange
⊠	743	302	0113	tangerine
∽	775	1031	1014	light blue
▼	905	257	1412	dark green
I	966	206	1209	lt sea green
☾	3811	1060	1101	turquoise

★ **Backstitch in one strand**

	926	850	1707	petrol blue

★ **STITCH COUNT** - 55 high x 45 wide

DAFFODILS KEY

★ **Cross stitch in two strands**

	DMC	Anchor	Madeira	
t	165	278	1414	light green
◣	562	209	1213	sea green
▽	704	255	1308	green
⋆◌⋆	727	293	0110	yellow
◤	742	303	0201	orange
⊠	743	302	0201	tangerine
∽	775	1031	1014	light blue
▼	905	257	1412	dark green
I	966	206	1209	lt sea green
−	3078	292	0102	light yellow
☾	3811	1060	1101	turquoise

★ **Backstitch in one strand**

	926	850	1707	petrol blue

★ **STITCH COUNT** - 58 high x 45 wide

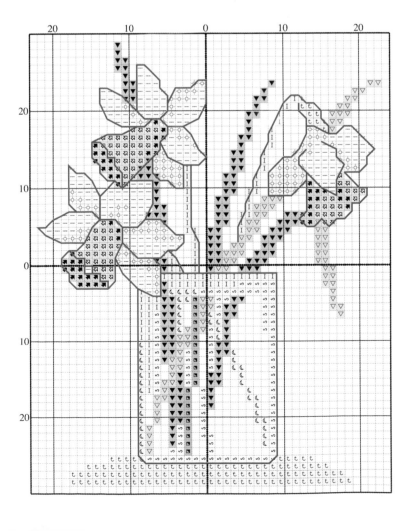

Summer Cottage

The second in our series of seasonal pictures, this picture shows old fashioned cottage-garden flowers arching around the house itself. There are foxgloves and poppies, michaelmas daisies and dog roses - all reminiscent of long, hot summer days

SUMMER COTTAGE KEY

★ **Cross stitch in two strands**

	DMC	Anchor	Madeira	
∩	blanc	2	2402	white
♀	150	1025	0508	cherry red
⚲	153	103	2712	light lilac
+	164	240	1209	light green
♦	300	352	2304	dark brown
■	310	403	2400	black
℮	333	119	0903	purple
e	340	118	0902	light purple
♥	349	13	0212	red
♡	350	11	0213	light red
3	605	1094	0613	pink
ь	612	832	2108	stone
b	644	830	1814	light stone
\	677	886	2207	sand
·ф·	726	295	0109	yellow
★	741	304	0202	orange
☆	742	303	0114	tangerine
?	760	1022	0405	dusky pink
ᷓ	772	259	1604	very lt green
◊	780	309	2213	topaz
⌁	792	177	0905	dark blue
A	818	23	0502	baby pink
▼	831	277	2201	dark khaki
▽	832	907	2509	khaki
∨	834	874	2510	light khaki
๑	904	258	1413	dark green
๑	988	243	1402	grass green
I	3078	292	0110	light yellow
☾	3607	87	0708	cerise
☾	3608	86	0709	light cerise
✸	3685	1028	0602	dark mauve
⌐	3747	120	0907	light violet
я	3776	1048	2306	ginger
◣	3799	236	1713	dark grey
$	3832	1024	0604	rose pink

★ Backstitch in one strand			
———	blanc	2	2402	white
———	300	352	2304	dark brown
———	904	258	1413	dark green

★ French knots in one strand			
●	988	243	1402	grass green
●	3607	87	0708	cerise
★ **STITCH COUNT** 133 high x 112 wide			

Winter Cottage

The fourth and final in our series of seasonal pictures, this design features the fruits and flowers of winter

Worked on a 14 count fabric, the completed design is about 33 cm (13 ins) wide and 28 cm (11 ins) tall.

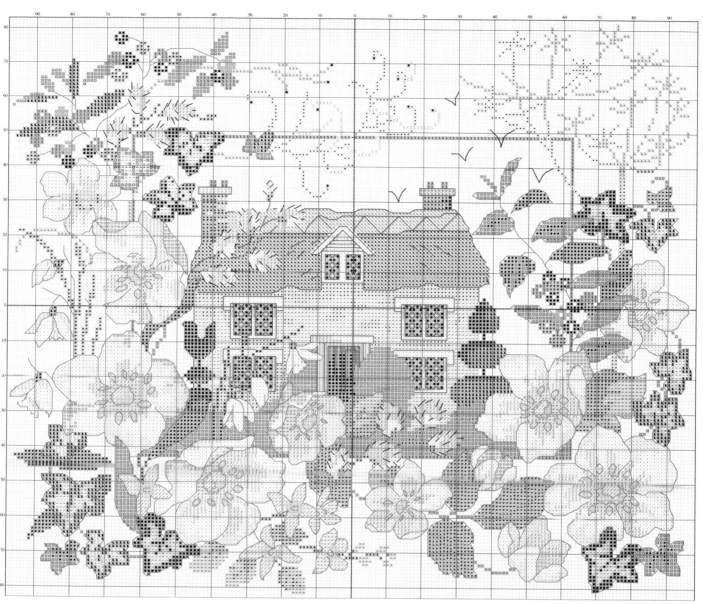

WINTER COTTAGE KEY

★ **Cross stitch in two strands**

	DMC	Anchor	Madeira	
·	B5200	1	2401	white
z	165	278	1414	lime green
■	310	403	2400	black
✹	319	1044	1313	bottle green
↜	470	266	1502	green
↖	611	898	2107	nut brown
I	648	900	1814	grey
+	676	891	2208	sand
●	720	326	0309	burnt orange
⌒	726	295	0109	yellow
-○-	728	305	0113	mustard
b	729	890	2209	dark sand
○	741	304	0202	tangerine
∽	745	300	0111	light yellow
♦	780	309	2213	dark topaz
▶	782	308	2212	topaz
\	819	271	0501	light pink

	DMC	Anchor	Madeira	
$	919	340	0313	terracotta
↗	937	268	1504	dk moss green
✿	988	243	1402	light green
3	3024	397	1901	light grey
⚲	3032	903	2002	beige
C	3047	852	2205	straw
K	3345	268	1406	dark green
♡	3779	868	2605	peach
♀	3799	236	1713	dark grey
♂	3819	278	2703	lime green
℮	3853	1003	0311	apricot

★ **Backstitch in one strand**

	DMC	Anchor	Madeira	
	B5200	1	2401	white
———	300	352	2304	dark brown
———	310	403	2400	black
———	3345	268	1406	dark green

★ **STITCH COUNT** 164 high x 194 wide

The beautiful picture shown below, and on the previous page, combines the tropical beauty of lilies, blossoms and a humming bird to great effect

Above: The chart for the large circular picture. The key is on the previous page.

Work on a 14 count fabric, this design is just under 22 cm (8½ ins) in diameter.

To increase the size of the design, work it on a lower count fabric. On an 11 count fabric, it will increase in size to about 28 cm (11 ins) in diameter.

To decrease the size of the design, work it on a higher count fabric. On a 22 count fabric, the design will become about 14 cm (5½ ins) in diameter.

If you use a very high or low count fabric, remember that you may need to use more or less strands of embroidery thread to match the size of the stitches. On a very high count fabric, you may need to use just one strand of thread, but on a lower count fabric you may need to use 3 strands.

Art Deco Alphabet

Personalise your possesions with this stylish alphabet — each and every letter is decorated with flowers in the art deco style. Use the subtle colours shown here, to create a soft and feminine effect, or bold and bright colours, to make a real impact. Work both initials, as we have here, or add just one — and they could be made to decorate a really special greeting card, or to frame as a mini-picture

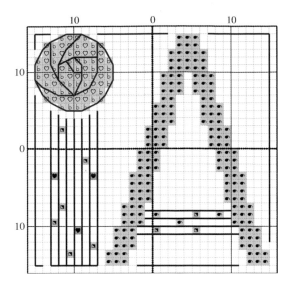

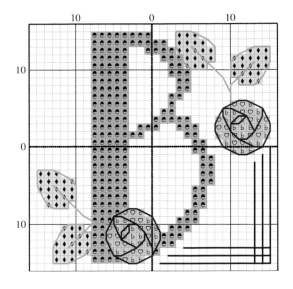

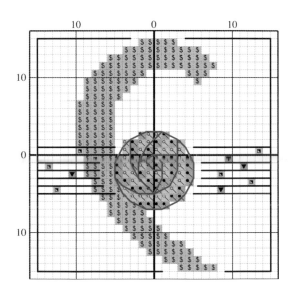

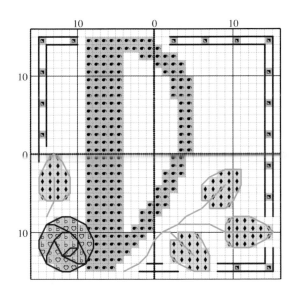

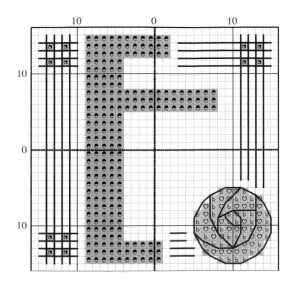

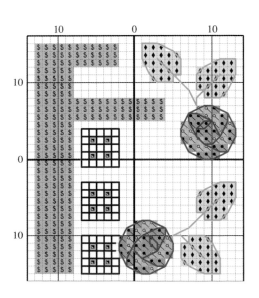

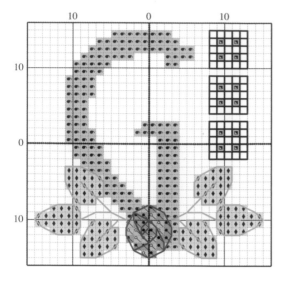

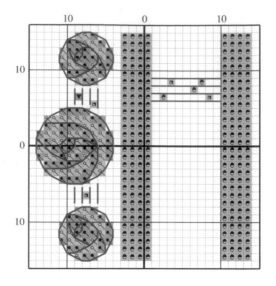

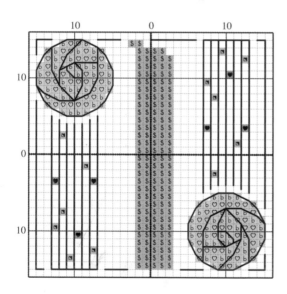

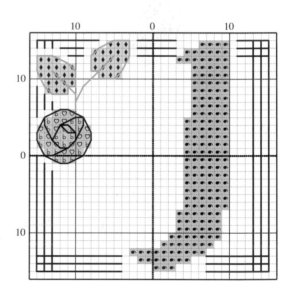

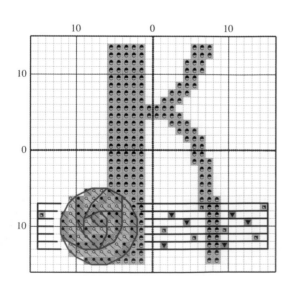

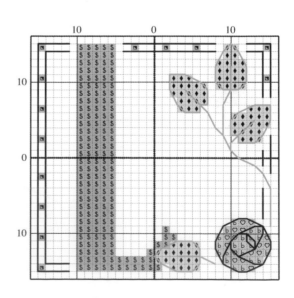

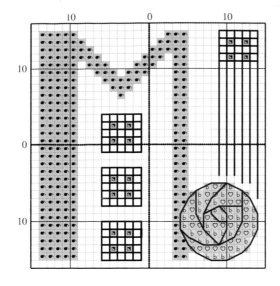

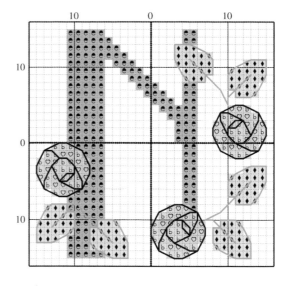

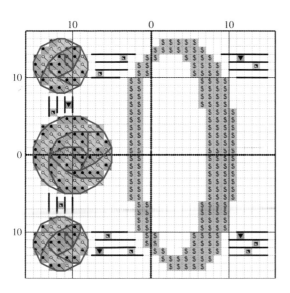

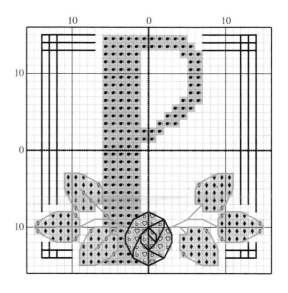

The key for all the letters is shown right.

The charts for letters A to E are shown on the previous page, letters G to P are here, and letters Q to Z are shown overleaf.

Worked on a 14 count fabric, each letter is about 5 cm (2 ins) tall. The widths vary depending on the letter worked.

ART DECO ABC KEY				
★ **Cross stitch in two strands**				
	DMC	Anchor	Madeira	
$	160	939	0906	blue
◪	317	400	1714	grey
▼	333	119	0903	purple
◕	518	1039	1106	turquoise
♥	917	89	0706	dark magenta
◔	926	850	1707	petrol blue
◆	993	1070	1111	mint green
♡	3608	86	0709	light mauve
◥	3731	76	0603	dark pink
◞	3733	75	0605	pink
b	3836	90	2713	mauve
★ **Backstitch in one strand**				
——	317	400	1714	grey
——	333	119	0903	purple
——	562	217	1205	dark green
——	917	89	0706	dark magenta
★ **STITCH COUNT** - 30 high x 30 wide				

Bluebell

ART DECO FLOWERS KEY (ALL)

★ Cross stitch in two strands			
	DMC	**Anchor**	**Madeira**
⌢	1	B5200	2401	white
★	327	100	0805	dark mauve
⚐	333	119	0903	purple
☆	340	118	0902	light purple
○	341	117	0901	violet blue
☾	347	1025	0407	red
◆	501	878	1704	dark mint
℧	562	217	1205	green
◊	563	215	1207	light green
☾	815	44	0513	dark red
✿	3328	1024	0406	light red
♥	3687	79	0604	dark plum
♡	3688	66	0605	plum
▽	3743	869	2611	grey mauve
★ **Backstitch in one strand**			
——	327	100	0805	dark mauve
★ **French knots in one strand**			
●	535	1041	1809	dark grey
●	729	890	2209	dark straw
★ **STITCH COUNT** - 78 high x 50 wide			

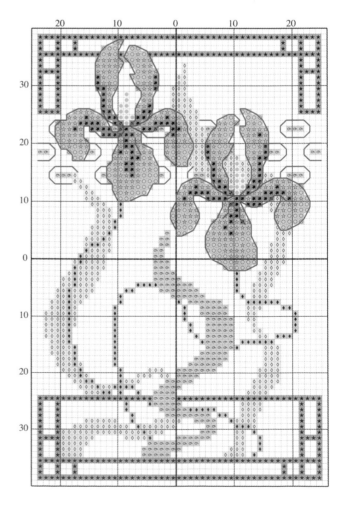

Water lily

Worked on a 14 count fabnric, all four art deco style flower designs are about 13 cm (5 ins) wide and 15 cm (6 ins) tall.

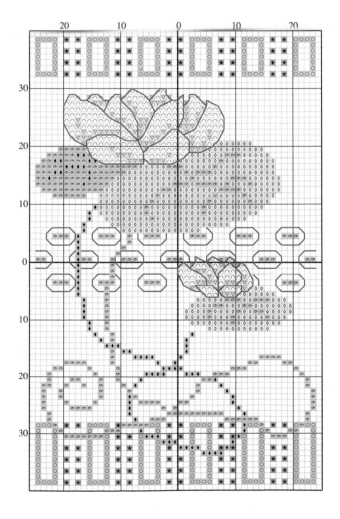

Bluebells & Poppies

*Make these bold greeting cards, featuring stunning
poppies or bluebells framed in toning colour card mounts —
they are bound to make an impact!*

Top below: The chart for the poppy design, shown bottom left in photograph.

Right: The key for all charts – the two here and those shown overleaf.

Bottom: The chart for the bluebell design, shown top left in the photograph.

BLUEBELLS & POPPIES KEY

★ **Cross stitch in two strands**

	DMC	Anchor	Madeira	
e	760	1022	0405	pink
I	761	1021	0404	light pink
♀	989	241	1401	light green
♥	3328	1024	0406	dark pink
v	3348	261	1501	light green
■	3371	382	2004	dark brown
◓	3816	876	1703	sea green
⚐	3838	176	2702	dark blue
b	3839	175	0902	blue
s	3840	130	0907	light blue

★ **Backstitch in one strand**

	DMC	Anchor	Madeira	
——	3328	1024	0406	dark pink
——	3371	382	2004	dark brown
——	3838	176	2702	dark blue

★ **MAXIMUM STITCH COUNT**

56 high x 57 wide

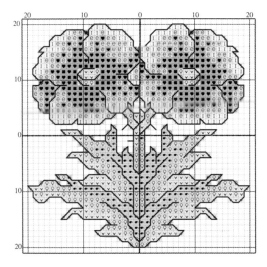

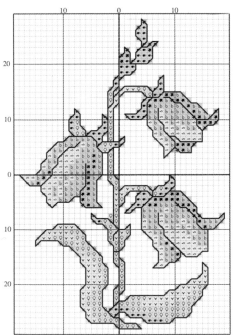

Sweet Rose

Few flowers could smell as sweet as roses - and you can re-capture their sweetness and their beauty with this stunning picture, complete with its classic quote!

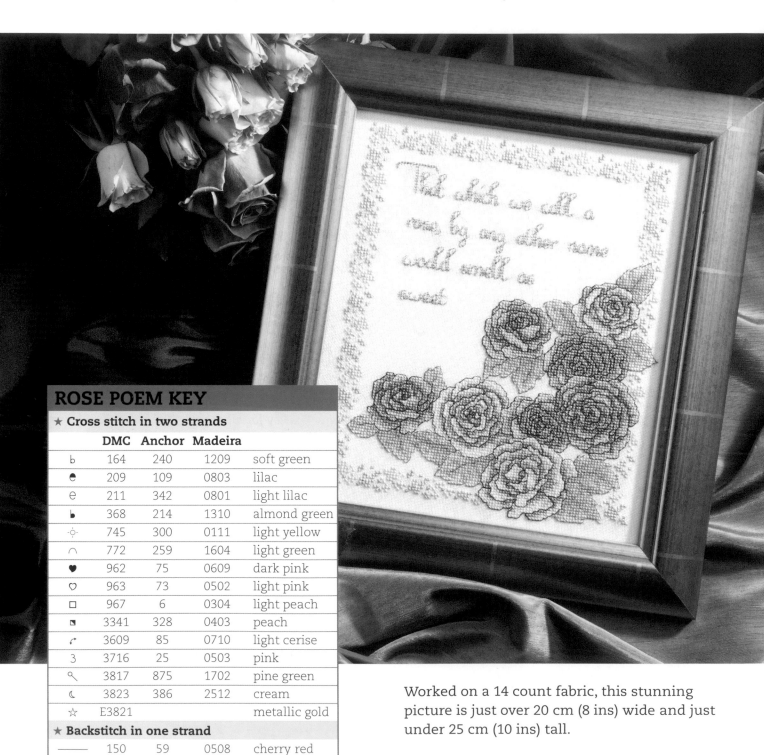

ROSE POEM KEY

★ Cross stitch in two strands

	DMC	Anchor	Madeira	
♭	164	240	1209	soft green
℮	209	109	0803	lilac
℮	211	342	0801	light lilac
♭	368	214	1310	almond green
☼	745	300	0111	light yellow
⌒	772	259	1604	light green
♥	962	75	0609	dark pink
♡	963	73	0502	light pink
□	967	6	0304	light peach
◨	3341	328	0403	peach
↶	3609	85	0710	light cerise
3	3716	25	0503	pink
⚲	3817	875	1702	pine green
☾	3823	386	2512	cream
☆	E3821			metallic gold

★ Backstitch in one strand

——	150	59	0508	cherry red
——	155	1030	0902	purple
——	367	217	1312	dark green
——	E3821			metallic gold

★ STITCH COUNT - 131 high x 109 wide

Worked on a 14 count fabric, this stunning picture is just over 20 cm (8 ins) wide and just under 25 cm (10 ins) tall.

The key is shown left, and the chart is opposite.

Beautiful Iris

*Re-capture the beauty of classic purple irises
with this stunning trio of designs*

DAISIES KEY

★ Cross stitch in two strands

	DMC	Anchor	Madeira	
·	blanc	2	2402	white
໑	704	237	1308	bright green
⟐	726	295	0109	yellow
w	910	228	1302	green
♡	963	73	0502	pink
☆	972	298	0107	dark yellow
◪	3834	100	0805	mauve
e	3844	410	1102	dark turquoise
e	3846	1090	1103	turquoise

★ STITCH COUNT 56 high x 56 wide

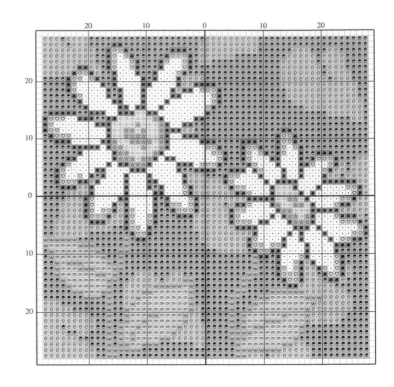

Above: The chart and key for the daisy design, shown top left in the photograph.

Below: The chart and key for the narcissi design, shown bottom left in the photograph.

Worked on a 14 count fabric, each design is just over 10 cm (4 ins) square.

DAFFODILS KEY

★ Cross stitch in two strands

	DMC	Anchor	Madeira	
·	blanc	2	2402	white
☾	210	108	0802	light lilac
◪	553	98	0712	lilac
໑	704	237	1308	bright green
⟐	726	295	0109	yellow
w	910	228	1302	green
☆	972	298	0107	dark yellow
+	3078	292	0102	light yellow
e	3857	936	2501	brown

★ STITCH COUNT 56 high x 56 wide

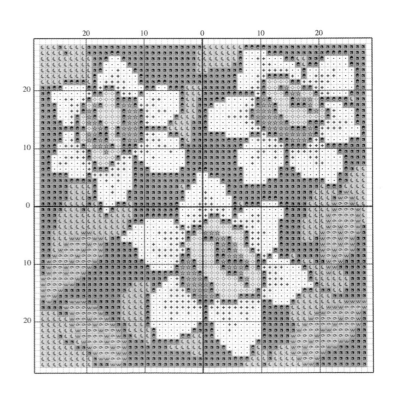

ANEMONES KEY

★ **Cross stitch in two strands**

	DMC	Anchor	Madeira	
∨	340	118	0902	violet
◤	550	102	0714	dark mauve
N	603	55	0504	pink
၈	704	237	1308	bright green
w	910	228	1302	green
◣	3041	871	0806	antique mauve
♡	3609	85	0710	light plum
●	3746	1030	2702	purple
◸	3747	120	0907	light violet
♥	3805	63	0702	cyclamen pink
$	3806	60	0701	light cyclamen

★ **STITCH COUNT** 56 high x 56 wide

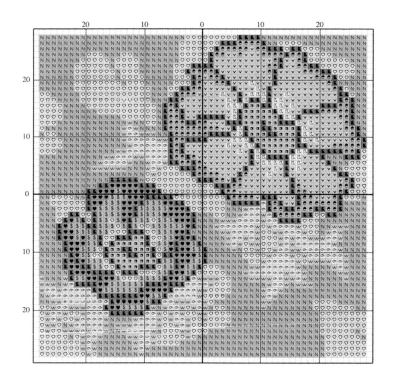

Above: The chart and key for the anemone design, shown top right in the photograph.

Below: The chart and key for the sunflower design, shown bottom right in the photograph.

SUNFLOWER KEY

★ **Cross stitch in two strands**

	DMC	Anchor	Madeira	
▼	301	1039	2306	tan
∨	340	118	0902	violet
●	400	351	2305	dark tan
◣	553	98	0712	mauve
၈	704	265	1308	bright green
☼	726	295	0109	yellow
✪	902	897	0601	dark plum
w	910	227	1302	green
+	3078	292	0102	light yellow

★ **STITCH COUNT** 56 high x 56 wide

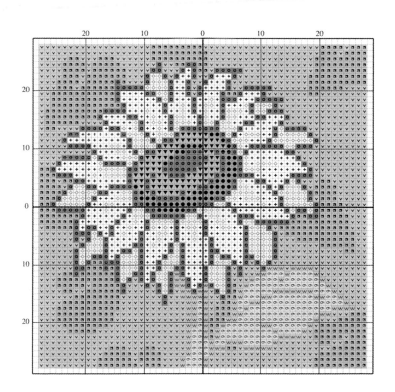

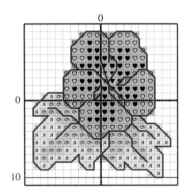

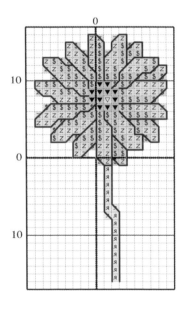

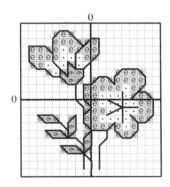

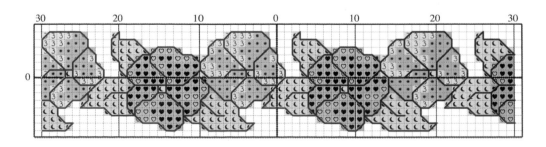

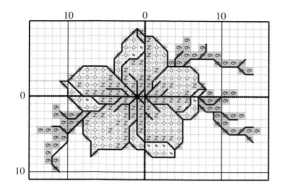

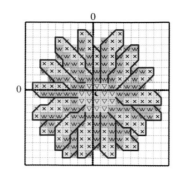

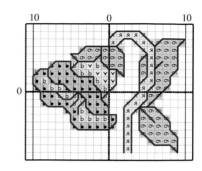

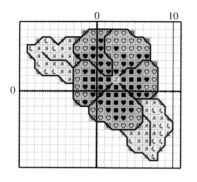

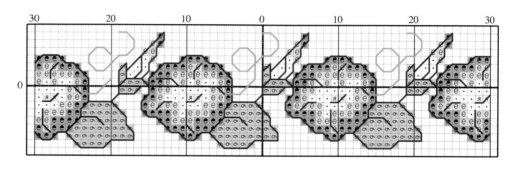

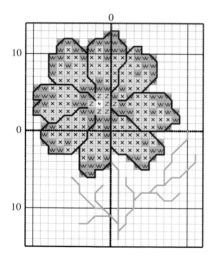

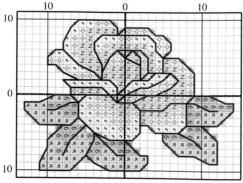

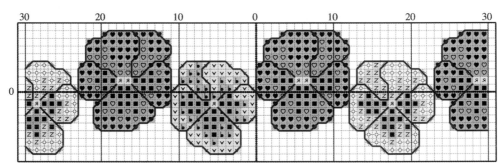

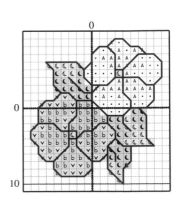

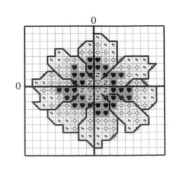

FLOWER QUICKIES KEY

★ Cross stitch in two strands

	DMC	Anchor	Madeira	
·	blanc	2	2402	white
b	208	111	0804	dark mauve
♭	209	109	0803	mauve
v	210	108	0802	light mauve
∽	320	215	1311	almond green
♥	349	13	0212	red
♡	351	10	0214	light red
я	368	214	1310	lt almond green
▽	436	1045	2011	tan
−	738	367	2013	light tan
$	741	304	00202	orange
∠	742	303	0114	dark yellow
-○-	744	301	0112	yellow
₥	745	300	0111	light yellow
3	760	1022	0405	dusky pink
◖	798	137	0912	dark blue
e	809	130	0909	blue
w	956	40	0506	bright pink
×	957	50	0504	pink
ᴧ	3072	847	1805	grey
*	3328	1024	0406	dk dusky pink
☾	3347	266	1408	green
☾	3348	264	1409	light green
■	3371	382	2004	dark brown
∩	3713	1020	0502	lt dusky pink
▼	3862	374	1913	light brown

★ Backstitch in one strand

——	3347	266	1408	green
——	3371	382	2004	dark brown

★ MAXIMUM STITCH COUNT
   34 high x 84 wide

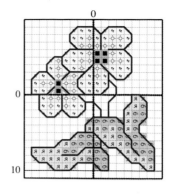

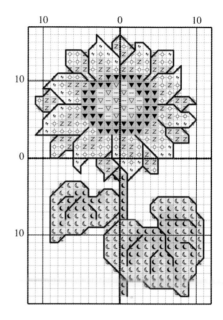

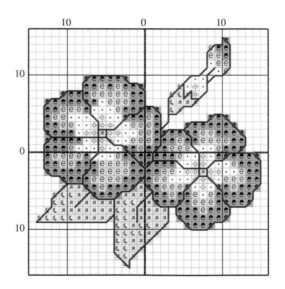

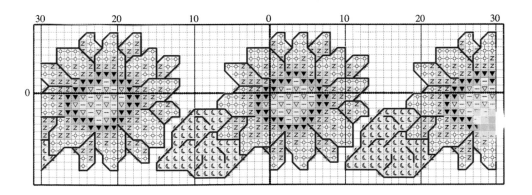

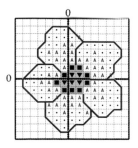

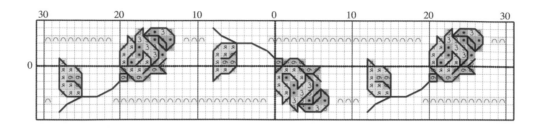

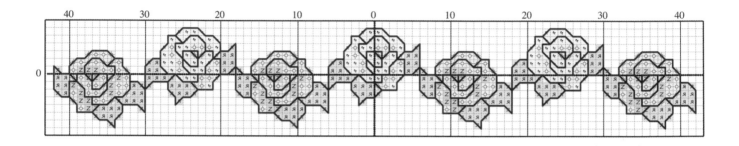